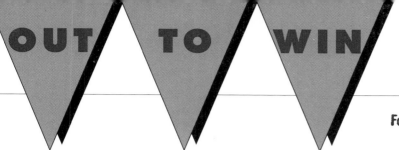

OUT TO WIN

Le Mans!

RACE AROUND THE CLOCK

BY JAY SCHLEIFER

CRESTWOOD HOUSE
PARSIPPANY, NEW JERSEY
Printed in U.S.A.

Published by Crestwood House, an imprint of Silver Burdett Press.
A Simon & Schuster Company
299 Jefferson Road, Parsippany NJ 07054

First Edition
Produced by Twelfth House Productions
Designed by R studio T

photo credits: cover, courtesy of Jaguar Photo Archives
courtesy of Collier Automotive Museum: 5, 9, 15, 17, 19, 26, 28, 32, 36
courtesy of the Bugatti Trust: 12
courtesy of Mercedes-Benz: 22-23, 42
name tk from jane Mason : 24
Jaguar Photo Archives: 40

Printed in the United States of America
10 9 8 7 6 5 4 3 2 1

LIBRARY OF CONGRESS CATALOGING-IN-PUBLICATION DATA
Schleifer, Jay
    Le Mans : race around the clock! / by Jay Schleifer.
        p.   cm.– (Out to win)
    Includes Index.
    ISBN 0-89686-820-6
    [1. Le Mans Endurance Race. France.   2. Automobile racing.]
    I. Title.   II. Series
    GV1034. 48. L4S35   1995
    796.7'2'0944–dc20   94-28497

CONTENTS

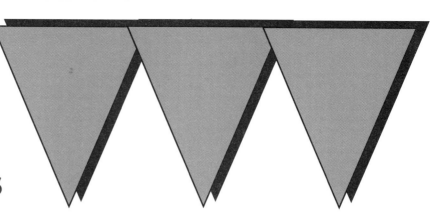

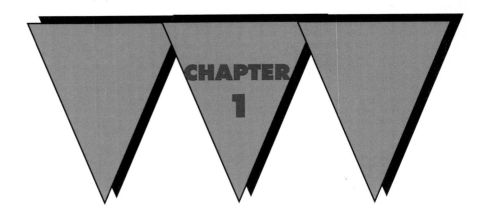

SATURDAY, 2 P.M.

Times like these make you wonder why you became a race car driver.

*It's the middle of the day. You're in France. And in just two hours you'll strap yourself into a **prototype** sports racing car—a car that's built to drive at speeds close to 250 miles per hour (mph).*

And this isn't an ordinary race. Because when the sun goes down this evening, you'll still be racing. Your wild ride will go right through the dark and dangerous night. And then it will go well into the next day. You'll be racing at sundown and sunup, no matter what the weather. For a few hours a co-driver will take over so you can rest. But other than that, you'll be at the wheel of this car for 24 straight hours.

Twenty-four hours on the track. And in this race, two hours on the track can tire a strong driver.

So why are you doing this?

It's what you've dreamed of doing for years—competing in the world's top sports car event, at Le Mans, France!

*Le Mans is to sports car lovers what Indy is to **open-wheel racers**. It's one of the truly great races. More than 70 years old, Le Mans gets more exciting every year.*

Porsche's 908 helped set the short-nosed, long-tailed look of the modern prototype. Note the trim tabs on the tail.

If you're out to win this amazing event, you need to know more about it. But we have some time before the race starts. So let's rev up with the story of Le Mans. Then we'll race around the clock!

CHAPTER 2

MAY THE BEST CAR WIN!

The year was 1923. Cars had been around for nearly 40 years, and they'd improved a lot during that time. But members of the Auto Club of Western France (or "ACO" from its French name, **Automobile Club de l'Ouest)** felt there was room for improvement.

For example, one ACO official was concerned about headlights. In those days car headlights were dim. In fact, they weren't much brighter than the lanterns carried by horse-drawn wagons. It was common for a driver to get into a nighttime accident because the headlights weren't bright enough to show what was ahead.

The ACO wanted to encourage carmakers to improve headlights and other electrical systems. So the club decided to sponsor a 24-hour **endurance** race. That way, carmakers would have to build stronger cars. The race would start in the late afternoon, run all night, and go on until the following afternoon. And it would be held rain or shine.

Besides pushing automakers to improve their cars, the race would bring publicity. A dramatic 24-hour race would help the club make news headlines. It might bring in new members, too!

There was just one question. Where would the race be held? ACO officials searched for the right course. It had to be straight enough so that drivers could go fast. It needed enough corners to be challenging. And it had to be close enough to a large city to attract a crowd.

The officials ended up *creating* the course they wanted. They used ordinary country roads that formed a loop just under 11 miles long. The course was on the outskirts of Le Mans, a city of more than 150,000 people southwest of Paris. Officials decided to call the race Les 24 Heures du Mans (The 24 Hours of Le Mans).

Actually, Le Mans had a history of speed even before the race. It had been the site of the world's first **Grand Prix** (Grand Prize) auto race. That race was staged by the ACO in 1906. Drivers went 12 laps around a 64-mile course.

Aviation history had also been made at Le Mans. When the Wright brothers wanted to sell their newly invented "aeroplane" to the French army, they set up an airfield at Le Mans to show the plane off. There's still a monument to the famous inventors on the outskirts of town. And there's a street named after Wilbur Wright. Later Le Mans served as a military airfield in both World War I and World War II. But nothing like the 24-hour race had ever been held there.

One new twist for that first race in 1923 was the rule book. The Auto Club wanted to make sure that all the cars developed for the track could also be sold to the public. So they created some rules:

▼ All cars had to be *exactly* like the ones you could order at the showroom. To be sure that all racers were real street models, carmakers had to present the officials with ten cars. Each one had to be exactly like the others. The officials decided which of the ten cars would make the run. That way, teams couldn't use a car that just *looked* like a street model.

▼ All but the smallest cars had to be four-seaters.

▼ Bags of sand were put in the backseat area so that the car would drive as if it carried a full load of passengers.

▼ The pit crew could not work on the car. It could only hand the driver tools and parts. Drivers had to fix any problems themselves.

▼ All convertible cars had to enter the pits on the fifth lap. Then the driver had to get out and put the top up, whether it was raining or not. On the twentieth lap, these cars had to stop again so the officials could make sure the top was still up.

This rule might sound a bit strange. But it made perfect sense to the officials of the ACO. They felt that the race should be like everyday driving. And everyday driving sometimes happened in the rain!

RUNNING START

The first 24-hour Le Mans was held on May 26-27, 1923. And as it turned out, it rained during the entire race. Thirty-three cars ran in this wet race, and 29 of them were French.

As expected, one of the French cars won. It was a Chenard & Walcker Sport. It covered more than 1,372 miles at an average speed of 57 mph. But among the "foreign" cars was an American Ford, entered by a Paris dealer. The car did well, finishing fourteenth. And Fords would do even better at Le Mans in the years to come.

The following year the Le Mans race was moved to June. Officials made this decision for two reasons: It rains less during June than during May, and the days are longer in June.

Le Mans is still a June event today. That doesn't stop the rain, though. Many races have been run under wet conditions.

As it turned out, most of the cars in the second Le Mans were French. But the winning car was a British Bentley. Today's Bentley is a leather-lined

Many of the signs at Le Mans are for French auto and parts companies. Renault builds cars. Cibie makes lights.

luxury cruiser built by the Rolls-Royce Company. But in the 1920s, Bentleys were monster-engined macho machines.

One famous Bentley was called the Blue Train Special. It raced the Blue Train, one of Europe's fastest railroad cars. The two machines raced across the European countryside in the early 1920s. The Bentley won.

Bentley was the first big winner of the Le Mans race. The dark green British bombers took not only the 1924 race. They also scored four more victories, in 1927, 1928, 1929, and 1930.

In its way, Bentley set a major Le Mans tradition—one brand of car winning again and again in just a few years. In later years, many car companies "owned" the race for short periods. Jaguar, Alfa Romeo, Mercedes-

Benz, Ferrari, Ford, and Porsche all had repeated Le Mans victories.

Other traditions also began in those early races. After the first race, organizers realized that the crowd couldn't be expected to watch cars go around and around for 24 hours. No matter how exciting the action got, 24 hours was too long. And the crowd couldn't even see the cars most of the time. Depending on the year, the track stretched between 8 and 11 miles. The cars passed any given point every 5-10 minutes.

So other excitement had to be provided. In 1924 the ACO staged a boxing match on the track grounds. Then a circus tent and carnival rides were added. In time, the infield of the track became a "village," complete with stores and restaurants.

Nowadays the "village" of Le Mans swells to nearly a quarter of a million people each June. Then the track sits almost empty the rest of the year.

The **Le Mans start** was invented in the 1920s, too. No longer used today, the start was based on the idea that drivers don't begin a road trip in their cars. They have to walk (or run) to their cars first.

For a Le Mans start, the cars were lined up on one side of the pit road, in angled parking spaces facing the track. The drivers lined up on the other side. Many crouched down like track-and-field runners waiting for the start of the 100-yard dash.

When the flag fell, the drivers sprinted to their cars. Then they daintily entered through the door (jumping into open cars was not allowed). Next they kicked the engine over. If a car started, the driver sped onto the track. If it didn't, the driver would grind the starter—while watching the other cars storm away.

Although drivers were supposed to put their seat belts on before driving off, many didn't take the time. Instead, as they whipped through the dangerous first curve, they belted with one hand and drove with the other. Many crashes happened in those first few seconds, perhaps because the drivers were doing two things at once.

The Le Mans start was dangerous for those who weren't fast runners. As these drivers crossed the track, they faced a thundering herd of 40 to 60 wild cars skidding around them!

Some drivers felt the start was unsafe, and they protested. Belgian star

Jackie Ickx, who won Le Mans seven times, chose not to run to his car when the flag fell. Instead, he stood around while the other drivers made their dash. When they were gone, he slowly shuffled across to his Porsche, climbed aboard, and started it up.

Ickx said it was silly to think that getting ahead in the first seconds of a 24-hour race would make a big difference in the outcome. In time, the rule makers came to agree with him. In 1970 the Le Mans start was replaced by a regular grid start.

Other Le Mans rules also changed over time. By 1925, the rule requiring convertible drivers to enter the pits and raise their tops was gone. It was replaced, though. The new rule made the drivers raise their tops at the starting line. Now drivers were running around their cars just seconds before the race began!

Rules aside, those first Le Mans races were spectacular. One reason was that the track itself was exciting. It had a tricky combination of tight turns and long straights. Parts of the track even became famous. Racing fans talked about the action at "Maison Blanche" ("White House") or at the turn called Arnage. Thousands of pictures were taken of cars passing under the Dunlop Bridge—a bridge used by fans to cross the track from the entrance to the infield. The bridge looked like a giant racing tire. But more than anything, the fans talked about the **Mulsanne Straight**.

Over 3 miles long, the Mulsanne is the longest straight run in big-time racing. It's three times as long as the straight on the back of the Daytona 500 track. On most straights, cars have to slow down for a turn before they've reached full speed. But the Mulsanne gives them enough room to show what they've got in an all-out blast of speed.

These days, that means well over 200 miles per hour. In fact, some cars have been clocked on the Mulsanne at 240 mph!

In those first races, drivers and carmakers learned that raw power is important at Le Mans. A fast car could build an incredible lead on the Mulsanne. After that, it was almost impossible to overtake it in the turns.

By the 1931 race, other makes had caught up with Bentley. The new winner was an Italian machine called Alfa Romeo. Alfa took the race four years in a row.

By the late 1930s, the Le Mans crown was back in French hands. The legendary blue cars of Bugatti were winners in both 1937 and 1938.

By the end of the decade, all but one of the major car-building countries had several Le Mans victories to its credit. The country that didn't was the United States. But one American car had come close.

In 1928 an American-built Stutz ran neck and neck with the winning Bentley. The cars switched leads again and again for 19 of the 24 hours. Then the Stutz had gearbox trouble. Although it kept jumping out of high gear, the big American machine still managed to come in second. It finished just 8 miles behind the Bentley in a race of more than 1,000 miles.

French fans loved it when their nation's Bugattis ran at Le Mans. These are early "Bug" racers.

CHAPTER
4

SATURDAY, 4 P.M.

Your start is about to happen. But you won't have to run to your car as the old-timers at Le Mans used to do. In a way, though, you've been running to get to Le Mans ever since you drove your first sports car.

If you'd grown up in the 1950s or 1960s, that car would have been a rickety, wire-wheeled English MG or Triumph. Or perhaps one of the old Porsches that looked like a turtle. But your first car was probably a hot little Honda CRX Coupe, an RX-7 Mazda, or even an older Corvette.

Whatever it was, it was nothing like the sedans most people drive. It was quick and nimble. It was as balanced as a ballet dancer. But it had the punch of a prizefighter. And its incredible handling made up for its smallish engine.

*In time, you met other sports-car owners and began racing. Your first races were against the clock and a forest of orange cones in a parking lot. This event was called **Autocross**. You drove as fast as you could through the curvy path outlined by the cones.*

Shortly after that you, took to the track. First you drove in local club races, where you found you had the talent to win. Now the little "toy" made way for special racing machinery.

Finally you got your big chance. A car owner hired you for the big 12-hour race at Sebring, Florida, and then for the Rolex 24-hour race at Daytona.

You placed well in both. The next year you were off to Le Mans.

Now you're here, about to drive a finned, bubble-topped 700-horsepower rocket on wheels. It's more car than you've ever handled. And you'll soon find out if you've got what it takes to drive it.

Since the track opened, fans have poured in from around the globe. More than 300,000 people are here. The sweet smell of French bread hangs in the air. The rock music is blaring.

In the garage areas, though, there's no time for partying. The mechanics have worked hard to get their cars ready on time.

Just before the start, there's a huge parade down the pit straight. Every one of the 50 driving teams is introduced to the crowd.

Then, shortly before 4 P.M., the French Auto Club president makes a speech. You don't understand a word of it, but it must have been the signal to start your engine. Because all of a sudden thousands of horsepower roar to life.

It's time to go.

You climb into your car and pull down the hatch-like door. You lock your seat belt and wait for the officials to wave you off. All around you are French, German, and English supercars like yours. And there's a herd of smaller machines. You're all rolling out of the pits in two multicolored lines. The lines of cars weave back and forth as drivers warm up their tires.

*The **pace car** leads the noisy, colorful pack of pavement-sniffing monsters. When they're up to speed, the pace car dives out of the way. Just as the clock strikes 4, the start signal falls.*

Everyone drag-races for the first corner. Somehow you all make it through safely. Then it's under the Dunlop Bridge and through the esses. And finally you go around the sharp right called Tertre Rouge (in French, Tertre Rouge means "Little Red Hill"). Now the Mulsanne is right ahead.

In a few seconds you're on the most famous straight in racing. You open the throttle wide and feel the thrill of going over 225 mph.

*The two kinks, or **chicanes**, that were recently put in the straight barely slow you down. But the hairpin curve that ends the Mulsanne does. After* the turn, you head into the **Indy** and Arnage curves and the second half of the course.

    Moments later, you swing past the pits and the start/finish.

    One lap down.

    No one can say what's waiting in the more than 350 laps yet to come. But you'll soon find out.

Racing is only part of the action. Fans can head for the carnival when the cars are out of view.

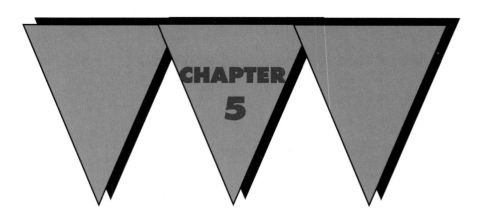

THE CADILLAC ADVENTURE

When World War II broke out, the French government turned Le Mans into an air force base. When the Germans overtook France, they used it for the same purpose. Nazi warplanes actually used the famous Mulsanne straight as a runway.

But a 3-mile-long piece of historic racetrack makes a good target for bombers. And before long, U.S. and British planes were blasting holes in the famous pavement. By the time the war ended, parts of the track looked like the surface of the moon.

The ACO couldn't start rebuilding the track until February 1949. But the job went well. When June rolled around, the race cars were rolling, too. But Le Mans had changed from the prewar years.

Over time, the cars had become less and less like street models. Now the ACO finally gave in to that trend. Beginning with the 1949 event, there was a new class of racers called prototypes. A prototype is an experimental car, very different from cars on the street. It wasn't long before the prototype ruled at Le Mans.

The idea of making Le Mans racers like street models hadn't entirely died, however. Even the prototypes had to have two seats and space for luggage. Officials tested the space with a special suitcase.

Designers quickly showed what they thought of these rules. The second seat in the prototypes was just big enough for a large dog. And the area around it was often filled with hot-water pipes and air ducts. Designers also took liberties with the luggage space. One prototype had no room inside the body. So car builders strapped a compartment just big enough to hold the suitcase to the rear of the car!

Among the entries in the 1949 race was a new Italian make that didn't exist before the war. The company's name was Ferrari. Its cars were fire red—the right color for cars that burned up the track!

When the starting flag fell, a two-time winner named Luigi Chinetti was at the wheel of one of the new Ferraris. He was also there when the checkered flag fell, and for almost all the time between. Chinetti won the 1949 Le Mans.

Most Le Mans entries have two or even three drivers. They take turns at the wheel. No one is expected to drive for 24 hours. But in a superhuman effort, Chinetti drove 23 of the 24 hours! No one has ever been able to

American Briggs Cunningham built cars around Cadillac and Chrysler engines. This bruiser was the C-4RK.

match Chinetti's performance.

Briggs Cunningham would have been happy to match Chinetti's win. Cunningham was a rich American whose interests included all kinds of racing. On the water, Cunningham captained a yacht that won the famed America's Cup. On land, he dreamed of winning Le Mans. But not with just any driver or in any car. Cunningham wanted to win Le Mans with an American driver in an American car.

Finding good U.S.-born drivers was no problem. But finding a car was. In the early 1950s, no U.S. maker built anything that could keep up with a Ferrari. But Cunningham decided to give one of America's finest makes a try. He prepared two cars for the 1950 race.

As the cars lined up for the start, Le Mans fans were treated to an amazing sight. In the midst of a field of hot Ferraris, Jaguars, and other sports machines stood a fully stocked Cadillac two-door coupe.

The Caddy had been repainted blue and white, the U.S. racing colors. And it carried racing numbers on the doors. But otherwise it looked like something a wealthy business executive would drive to the golf course. It had tail fins, chrome bumpers, and a "flying lady" statue perched on the hood.

Racing fans laughed . . . and Cunningham went right along with the joke. He dressed his drivers in business suits and ties. In fact, the Cadillac was all business, and its business was racing. Its engine had been hot-rodded. Heavy-duty brakes and shocks had been bolted into place.

Cunningham's other car had no tail fins but was just as wild. He had wrapped a squarish body around another Cadillac engine and chassis. The car was so strange-looking that the French began calling it Le Monstre. Cunningham would drive this monster himself.

From the moment the race began, both Caddys were in the chase. As Cunningham had projected, powerful American V-8s were perfect for Le Mans's long straights and swoopy curves. And the cars' "Detroit Iron" chassis seemed unbreakable. Even when Le Monstre crashed hard into a sandbank, Cunningham just backed it out and kept on going.

As the hours wound on, both cars kept improving in the standings. A

The C-5R was one of the last Cunninghams. Notice how sleek it is compared with the C-4RK in the previous photo.

French Talbot, driven by the father-son team of Louis and Jean-Louis Rosier, was first to the flag. But the tail finned Caddy finished a strong eleventh out of 60 starters. And Le Monstre crossed the line in thirteenth place.

Cunningham had always known he'd need more than a hot rodded stock car to win Le Mans. He'd have to build cars especially for this kind of racing. But his Cadillac adventure proved that American parts and engines had what it took to power those special cars.

In the years that followed, Cunningham returned again and again with cars he had built himself. Through friends at Chrysler, he was able to get the company's mighty **hemi** V-8 engines. These engines were even stronger than the Cadillac's. From this point on, Cunningham's special cars would feature Chrysler power.

Starting with Model C-1, each Cunningham machine was brutally fast. Each car used aircraft-tubing frames, giant finned brakes, and streamlined bodies. And every year, the Cunningham racers got faster and faster.

The problem was that the European cars were improving, too. No matter what Cunningham did, one of the factory designs was always a jump ahead.

The team's best year was 1953, when Cunningham cars finished third and seventh. That year one of these cars also set the fastest speed in the race—almost 155 mph. But by the mid-1950s, Cunningham faced the fact that he could never match the time or money the big carmakers spent on racing. He closed his shop for good. But he'd become a part of Le Mans history. And the name Briggs Cunningham remains one of the most honored in motor racing.

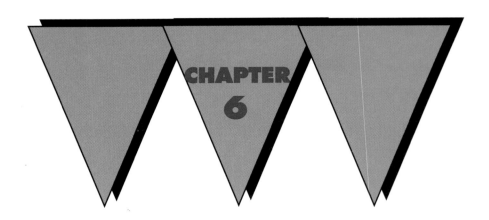

CHAPTER 6

BIG CATS AND GULLWINGS

While Cunningham was trying to build a winning machine, Mercedes-Benz and Jaguar were controlling the 1950s Le Mans races.

The German founders of Mercedes-Benz had invented the automobile back in 1883. Maybe that's why the company seemed to beat everyone whenever it hit the tracks.

In 1952 Mercedes decided to enter Le Mans. And the 300SL was the car it chose to race. This high-speed coupe was the first car to be built with a space frame. This frame was made of dozens of tiny, incredibly strong metal tubes. These tubes replaced the usual thick steel rails. The design saved huge amounts of weight. But it made it impossible to have the usual swing-out doors, because tubes filled the space where the bottom of a door would usually go. So Mercedes built doors that swung up, like a bird's wings. These doors gave the 300SL coupe its famous nickname—the Gullwing.

A Gullwing flew to victory in the 1952 Le Mans, much to the dismay of the British company Jaguar.

Jaguar's first Le Mans was the 1952 race, and it drove a C-Type car with a powerful 6-cylinder engine called the XK. Although Jaguar lost, the company had a surprise in store for the racing world. In 1953 the British company introduced the world's first automotive **disk brakes**.

Until the C-Type, all racers used **drum brakes**. Drum brakes stop a car by moving the parts inside a closed drum that's attached to the wheels. When the driver pushes the brake pedal, the parts press against the inside of the drum, slowing it down. The wheel attached to the drum slows down, too. The design is simple, and it works. But on rainy days, water splashes into the drum and makes the parts slip. Also, when brakes are used hard, they produce heat. The drums trap the heat inside, warping the parts and weakening the braking power.

Disk brakes work like the brakes on a 10-speed bicycle. Finger-like grippers grab and squeeze the wheel from both sides until it stops. (On a car, they actually grab a disk attached to the wheel.) There is no closed drum to hold water or heat. The brakes stay drier and cooler, and they work better.

Jaguar installed the new brakes in a C-Type. And the results blew drivers of other cars away! In one race, British superstar Stirling Moss was at the wheel of a disk-brake-equipped Jag. Fellow driver and friend Rudi Caracciola (Kah-rah-SEE-oh-lah) was driving a bigger, more powerful Mercedes.

"We caught up with Rudi," said Moss, "and for about 60-70 miles, we were able to outbrake him every time! He'd start to slow for a corner, and expect us to do the same, but we went by him flat out, *then* put the brakes on in front of him. He said it was incredible! Several times, he didn't think my car was going to stop!"

The Jag didn't stop—winning, that is. A C-Type took the 1953 race. Then, in 1954, an even more advanced racer, the D-Type, hit the tracks. The D added superstreamlined design to the C's power and braking. And it was built in an entirely new way.

Instead of the usual body bolted to a frame, the D's body *was* its frame. Just as on an airplane, tightly stretched metal panels gave the racing car all the strength that it needed. There was no need for a heavy steel skeleton underneath.

    But even with the new car, 1954 was not to be Jaguar's year. Ferrari appeared with a superpowerful motor. It proved that go power could still beat stopping power. The Italian stallions simply outran the Jags.

    But fans and Jaguar people suspected foul play, as all the Jags came down with coughing fits. Their fuel lines were clogged with sand! No one ever proved it was more than just bad luck. The D's day would come soon enough, though.

    In 1953 and 1954 Mercedes-Benz turned its attention to open-wheel machines. But a return to Le Mans was planned for 1955.

    When Mercedes returned in 1955, it raced the 300SLR, a car that was even faster than the 300SL. One new feature was racing's first **air brake**. This giant metal panel popped open behind the driver's head whenever the car had to slow down in a hurry. The air brake caught the air like a

The C (#19) and D (#17) Jaguars marked the first use of disk brakes and better streamlining at Le Mans.

parachute and held the car back.

Fans still remember these giant flaps rising and falling as the 300SLRs circled the track. They made mincemeat of the other cars for the first hours of the race.

Then at 6:29 P.M.—two and a half hours into the race—tragedy struck.

A D-Type Jag passed a slower Austin-Healey on the narrow straight in front of the pits. Then the Jaguar cut in front of it. This forced the slow car onto the left side of the track, where the faster cars usually race.

At that moment, Mercedes-Benz driver Pierre Levegh was pushing hard in his silver 300SLR on the left side of the track. Suddenly the slower car was directly in his path.

As former driver John Fitch tells it, "Levegh threw up one arm to warn those behind him. Then he braked and tried to slip between the slower car and an earth bank. He didn't make it."

The Mercedes hit the left rear tire of the Austin-Healey, forcing the SLR upward and throwing it onto the top of the bank. It struck a concrete wall and exploded. The blast sent parts of the car flying into the crowd, killing over 80 people. Levegh died with them. It was the worst accident in the long history of motor racing.

As smoke rose from the burning wreck, the race went on. Nobody was sure what had happened. First, it was thought 3 or 4 had died. But, sadly, the number soon climbed to 40.

"It was a long time until we realized how awful it was," Stirling Moss (now driving for Mercedes) said later. "At about 2 in the morning, we got the word from Germany to pull out of the race."

Even though a Mercedes was leading at the time, the silver cars left the track. They did not return to racing for another 30 years.

A D-Type Jaguar went on to win this saddest of Le Mans races. But the British builder took no pride in the prize. Jaguar never even mentioned the victory in its ads. The company won Le Mans again in both 1956 and 1957. But after the 1957 season, Jaguar left racing, too.

The great Le Mans crash of 1955 caused big changes in motor racing. Le Mans was rebuilt. Roads in the pit area were widened. Fences were put up so that fans were farther away from the track. The rules were rewritten to slow the cars down. And at least one top driver, Phil Walters, quit racing.

CHAPTER 7

SUNDAY, 3 A.M.

As your car roars past the pit area for the 220th time, you think about the brutal 1955 accident. Luckily, the night has gone smoothly. There haven't been any major accidents—just the usual number of breakdowns.

A Porsche 962 pits for engine work. Note the steering wheel on the *right* side.

A few hours ago, at 10 P.M., you stopped in the pit for a driver change. One of your teammates took over while you caught some much-needed sleep.

You'd always wondered how drivers could sleep with bright lights on and racing engines roaring. But you found it was easy. You were out as soon as your head hit the cot. Then, at 3 A.M., the burst of noise from your car pulling in said it was time to get back in the saddle.

Now you're back out here, and you understand what it means to be truly alone. You can see flashes of light in the infield from time to time. But mostly your world has become a black tunnel. And you're hurtling through that tunnel at close to 200 mph.

CHAPTER
8

RED TIDE

When Jaguar and Mercedes moved out of the Le Mans winner's circle, Ferrari moved back in. The big red Italian cars were the kings of racing in the early 1960s. They won with sports cars and with Grand Prix open-wheelers. It seemed that nobody could catch them.

Ferrari began to prove its strength almost as soon as the last D-Type Jag boarded the truck for home. A Ferrari won the 1958 race. Then the red

This Ferrari "LM" (Le Mans) model raced in the GT class. GTs are more like street machines than the wilder prototypes.

machines finished in six of the seven top places in 1960. In 1961 the Ferraris won again.

The red tide swept away every other car on the track. During the Ferrari years, the Italians scored a record nine Le Mans victories. That was almost twice as many wins as Jaguar.

But right in the middle of it all, a lone British car took the 1959 Le Mans. And it was one of the greatest races ever.

28

The car was an Aston-Martin, whose company had been trying to win at Le Mans for 30 years. The first Aston ran in 1928, and the company had hardly missed a year. But while Aston had plenty of spirit, it just didn't have the power to win Le Mans.

Three of Aston's green machines entered the 1959 Le Mans. But everyone knew that even Aston's best was slower than the Ferraris.

As the race began, it became clear that the British team had a game plan in mind. Driving ace Stirling Moss (yes, he did have a knack for picking the best brand!) took off like a scared rabbit. He was racing much too fast for his car to last 24 long hours. And everybody knew it.

The car wasn't supposed to last. It was supposed to lead the Ferrari team on a merry chase. The idea was that they'd get the drivers on the Italian team to push their cars too hard.

For several hours Moss poured it on. His car gave all it had in the battle. The Ferraris charged down the track after Moss, without considering what the chase was doing to their engines.

In time, the Aston gave out, and two of the red cars took the lead. But at 2 A.M., one of the two leading Ferraris suddenly began having gearbox troubles. Then, the next afternoon, the other one started to overheat. Chasing Moss had taken precious hours off both car's lives.

It was time for the British to spring their trap. The other two Aston drivers had been following orders by lying back. Their cars still had plenty of go. Now they poured on the power! As the front-running Ferrari died in a cloud of steam, the Astons grabbed the lead. Two hours later, an Aston crossed the finish line—winner at last—after 30 years!

As the 1960s wore on, Le Mans lost some of its excitement. There was Ferrari, and then there was everyone else. Fans eagerly looked forward to a new challenger to give the Italians a run for their money.

But where would the next challenge come from? The answer would surprise the world!

THE FORD-FERRARI WAR

I n far-off Detroit, the Ford Motor Company was known as a builder of family cars. But it was trying to change its image. It wanted to have a reputation for designing performance cars. The quickest way to create that reputation, Ford thought, was to win some races.

The company decided to support **NASCAR** stock car racing. It also entered the Indy 500. Victories in these races would make Ford cars famous in the United States. But as a worldwide company, Ford also had to win the world's biggest race. That race was Le Mans.

There was one problem. In its 60 years in business, Ford had never produced a real sports car. But Ford executives thought they had a solution. They would use Ford's bottomless supply of money to buy a company that built sports cars. Then they would put the Ford name on those cars. They even had the perfect car company in mind—Ferrari!

For several months in 1963, Ford executives talked with Enzo Ferrari. Ferrari had been interested in getting out of the business end of automaking. He wanted to spend all his time building race cars. Selling the company would let him do that. Ferrari also wanted the millions of dollars Ford was offering him.

But Ford had so many rules, contracts, and lawyers. Ford was a huge

30

company. Would Enzo Ferrari have to sign a time card to get his paycheck? He was used to being his own boss. After several months of negotiating, Ferrari showed the Ford executives the door.

When Henry Ford II heard this, he was furious. He decided it was time to teach this haughty Italian a lesson. He vowed that he would beat Ferrari on the racetrack. And the chief battleground would be Le Mans.

The Ford-Ferrari war, as it was called, began in 1963. Ford had found a small British maker called Lola. The company had a promising sports car design. Ford bought the Lola design. Then a worldwide team of Ford people improved the car to make a real racing machine. The car was called the Ford GT40, because it was 40 inches high.

The first GT40s rolled onto the Le Mans track in June 1964. They were blindingly fast—faster even than the Ferraris in a short burst of speed. In fact, a Ford actually led the race for the first hour. But the U.S. carmaker's lack of experience showed. At high speeds, air got under the cars, and the GT40s started to lift off the ground! They were almost uncontrollable. At the finish of the 1963 race, Ferraris came in first, second, and third. There wasn't a GT40 in sight.

The Americans learned from their mistakes, however. A year later, in 1965 an improved GT40 was back. So was a new kind of GT40. Called the Mark II, it had a far bigger engine.

The first GT40 had been powered by a 5-liter V-8. But the Mark II featured a 7-liter monster. Ford used this engine in its NASCAR stock car racers back home.

The Mark II could easily exceed 200 mph on the Mulsanne Straight. And it was solidly built. Both the improved GT40 and the Mark II had new bodies that would keep them firmly grounded to the track.

The Ford team had grown in numbers. Six GT40s were on the course. And team manager Carroll Shelby had brought another car—the Cobra (a small, lightweight car with a powerful V-8 engine)—to the race.

Ferrari was not about to give in easily. No less than 11 of the Italian supercars showed up to meet the American challenge. Even though the Fords were faster, Ferrari knew that nobody controlled racing luck. Once the race began, anything could happen.

31

Fords in the lead. This was a familiar sight at Le Mans in the mid-1960s.

It did. Within hours, the U.S. team could see its hopes turning to disaster. GT40s were dying all over the track. By dawn the next day, the only Ford left running was one lonely Cobra.

Ferrari also suffered from the long night's racing. Eight of its cars had died in action. But the three that survived finished first, second, and third. It was Ferrari's ninth Le Mans win.

Both warriors went home for the winter to rebuild their armies and sharpen their weapons. When Le Mans opened in 1966, Ferrari returned with a strong force—and found that 13 Fords were lined up on the track.

Suddenly, though, Ford had another car to beat. A rich Texan named Jim Hall had been having success with a racing machine he had built himself. The car, called a Chaparral, was powered by a Chevrolet V-8 engine.

Perhaps Ford's greatest fear was that their team would beat

Ferrari—only to be beaten by a Chevrolet!

As the race wore on, Ford after Ford died. But so did most of the Ferraris and the Chaparral. By the next afternoon, only three Fords were running. But they were running first, second, and third.

Ford executives suddenly felt sure they would win. They now began to talk about *how* they would win. Someone suggested it would make a great picture in the newspapers if the three cars crossed the line side by side by side in a dead heat!

Instructions went out to the drivers in their cars. The first-place driver, Ken Miles, had held a long lead for hours. Now he was ordered to slow down and let the other Fords catch up.

Then someone checked the rule book and learned that a dead heat was not possible at Le Mans. The car that had traveled the most distance would be named the winner, even if the difference was only a few feet.

In the end, Ken Miles came in second place. He lost the top spot because the car behind him—the one he'd let catch up—made a last-minute dash to the finish. That car beat Miles by a few feet. Miles was furious, but it did make for a great picture!

After three years of trying, Ford finally had its win at Le Mans. The following year, 1967, Ford returned with an even more powerful car, the Mark IV. It was driven by the American team of Dan Gurney and A. J. Foyt. For the second year in a row, Ford beat Ferrari. Proud of what it had done, the Ford factory team retired.

It was a proud day for Briggs Cunningham, too. Even though he had had no part in it, his longtime dream of an American driver winning in an American car had finally come true!

The Ford factory team was gone, but the GTs were not. The company had sold some of the cars to private owners. And those owners now went on racing their own GT40s.

And to make it even worse for Ferrari, privately owned Fords beat the red cars in both the 1968 and 1969 races. That gave Ford four victories in four years. It also buried Ferrari as the king of Le Mans.

But soon both Ford and Ferrari would lose their throne to a new king. And this king had magically transformed himself from a dwarf.

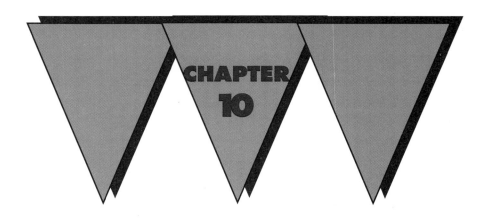

THE "DWARF OF STUTTGART"

Each year the big Ferraris, Fords, and Jaguars battled each other at Le Mans. But there was also another race going on. It was the Le Mans of the little cars—the MGs and Austin-Healeys, Renaults, and Sunbeams.

Smaller cars actually took up most of the track. They spent the 24-hour race zooming along in the right lane while the big machines whizzed by on the left. None of these pocket rockets stood a chance of winning the big prize. But they had their own prizes.

One of these prizes was called the **Index of Performance**.The index was a complex formula of engine size and distance traveled. The result was a number, not a checkered flag. And it didn't matter who crossed the finish line first. Instead, the calculators chewed up all the data, and then told you who'd won.

Often the index winner was a car the world had seldom heard of. The French Gordini was always a favorite for the index. A car called the DB also did well.

Another small-car prize was for the 2-liter-class win. At the time, the big cars were running engines from 4 to 7 liters.

The 2-liter class was won year after year by a German car. This car started out as little more than a hot-rodded Volkswagen. The car, which was built near the city of Stuttgart, was named after its designer, Porsche.

Each year, the little silver Porsches played their part in the great Le Mans drama. They looked like bumpy silver beetles. And their rear-mounted, **air-cooled engines** made a sewing-machine noise that was almost comical. One writer nicknamed Porsche the "Dwarf of Stuttgart."

But while fans laughed and other carmakers grabbed the headlines, Porsche was gaining experience. Before long, Porsche had one of the top teams at Le Mans. Unfortunately, few people noticed. Then something happened. In the middle of Ford's all-powerful sweep of Le Mans, the rule makers announced an important decision. Starting with the 1969 race, there would be a cap on engine size. Giant machines like the Ford GT40 would no longer be allowed. Now car companies that built smaller engines had a chance to win. The dwarf could become a king.

Porsche made the most of its opportunity. For several years the company had been at work on its first "win-it-all" Le Mans cars.

The model 908 was the first Porsche with an engine bigger than 2 liters. It featured a 3-liter, 8-cylinder **boxer** engine. The nickname came from the way the motor's cylinders were arranged. The cylinders were in two rows of four, opposite each other. When the engine was running, the cylinders seemed to jab at each other like boxers in a prizefight.

The 908 was only the first of the new breed. Next came the even more awesome model 917. It had a flat 12-cylinder engine that produced nearly 600 horsepower.

Star driver Vic Elford piloted the model 917 in one of the first tests. "I fell in love with the 917," he later said. "It was my sort of car . . . unbeliev-ably fast, with a fearsome reputation among other drivers. They'd see us in the mirrors and line up on the right to let us pass."

The incredible thing about the 908 and the 917 was that they were air-cooled. One small plastic cooling fan kept all those angry cylinders from blowing their gaskets—even on the hottest day in June.

But air cooling was also part of Porsche's winning edge. The cars didn't need radiators, water pumps, or hoses—so the car weighed less. And there were fewer parts to break. But just in case the fan wasn't enough, Porsche had a backup system. It sprayed a cooling mist of oil on the

The Porsche 917 was a 200-plus mph cruise missile that hardly slowed down in the dark and rain.

hottest parts.

Porsche had also done its homework in the **wind tunnel**. The 908 and 917 were sleek road huggers with short noses and long streamlined bodies. And Porsche borrowed a trick from aircraft science. Two flaps had been fitted to the rear of the body. They moved up and down like the trim tabs on an airplane's wings. The tabs used the force of wind to press the car to the road. This action was especially helpful in the turns. On the fast straights, the tabs released the wind pressure.

With their aerodynamic shape and the wind tabs, the Porsches could blast down the Mulsanne at more than 240 mph! The one-time "Dwarf of Stuttgart" had grown to awesome size.

The 1969 Le Mans race was a nail-biter. A GT40 Ford, driven by Le Mans ace Jackie Ickx, was able to eke out a win, finishing just ahead of the best-running Porsche. But Porsche roared back and took its first overall win in 1970, beating the cars in its class and the bigger machines.

A high-tech French car called the Matra took the race four times in the early 1970s. But after that, it was Porsche all the way. The 917 and its later models ran over everything in sight at Le Mans from the mid-1970s to the mid-1980s for the next 11 years. At times the world's greatest sports-car race became a Porsche Parade. One year, Porsches won nine of the first ten places!

Like all superstars, Porsche took some good-natured kidding. Some people compared the pink color of one team of Porsches to a pig. The Porsche drivers and mechanics had a comeback for that, though. Their car was painted up like a butcher's chart, with dotted lines showing the cuts of pork!

In spite of the jokes, Porsche deserved every victory it won. But victory for the same car became tiresome to many fans. They looked forward to a time when they could wonder again which car would win, not just which Porsche.

In a way, Porsche was allowed to win all those races. Only the largest carmakers could stop the German auto wonder. And many of those carmakers had pulled out of Le Mans.

One reason was that large companies were making important changes to their street models. In the 1970s gas prices skyrocketed. Buyers were demanding more economical cars. At the same time, new laws forced car-makers to build safety features into their vehicles and to pay attention to pollution control. With all of these changes taking place in the auto indus-try, there was little time left for racing.

Money was just as important as time when it came to building race cars. In any Le Mans race, one car usually broke down. Another might have an accident. That meant you needed at least a three-car team to have a chance to win. One top Porsche engineer put it this way: "In a battle like Le Mans, the number of warships counts."

Entering a multicar team could cost millions of dollars. This factor alone put many automakers out of the running. So the Porsche Parade continued.

SUNDAY, NOON

Ah, yes. The Porsches. There's one on your tail right now, and three in the pack ahead. But this is not the time to worry about them. Your job at the moment is to keep a steady pace of 150 mph. You and your teammate have kept that pace for 20 hours now. You'll have your chance to show what you can do in the last half hour of the race.

But suddenly, coming under the Dunlop Bridge for the 300th time, you spot trouble. Spinning, flying, colliding cars are all around you. It's the classic Le Mans accident—one of the Porsches has run into a slower machine.

You jerk the thick rubber rim of your steering wheel to the left—hard—and brake with all you've got. Your racer gets around most of the broken parts littering the road. But it just misses burying its streamlined nose in the sandbank. Then a giant thump underneath tells you you've rolled over something big. A sudden nonstop shaking from the steering wheel tells you your car is hurt. How badly? There's no way for you to know.

If this were yesterday, or last night, you'd pit and let the crew check things out. But you're in the homestretch now. You've got just hours to go. There's no time for a major repair. Just letting the crew look at the car would cost you valuable time. So you keep going—and hope the car hangs together until 4 P.M.

RISING SUN

In the early 1980s it looked as if the Porsche Parade at Le Mans was about to end. Jaguar had decided to get back into racing. So had Mercedes-Benz.

Jaguar and Mercedes had always used racing as a way to improve their cars. But there was another big reason for their return to racing. The Japanese were after their customers. Toyota and Nissan had begun to build cars in the same price class as Jaguar. The famous European companies were running scared. They had to convince buyers that their cars were winners.

Jaguar took the plunge first. For European racing, the famous English maker hooked up with a race shop called Tom Walkinshaw Racing (TWR). The cars Jaguar and TWR built together were known as the XJR series.

The XJR Jaguars were very advanced. Their undersides were formed into a series of wind tunnels. These tunnels created a vacuum-cleaner effect. The car was sucked down against the road so it stuck like glue through turns. This method of using airflow to improve handling is called **ground effects.**

Even with ground effects, Jaguar did not win Le Mans right away. It took three tries before the team was strong enough to take on the Porsches. And the XJR series was up to a ninth model by the time Jaguar entered a five-car team in the 1988 race.

The race itself was a tremendous duel. The winning Jag finished just two minutes ahead of the best running Porsche, after 24 hours of racing. After 30 years, the big cats of Jaguar had again proved their power on the world's top racetrack. But just barely. Except for one other Jag, which fin-

This Jaguar XJR-9 is totally different from the C- and D-Types that raced in the 1950s.

ished fourth, every other car in the top ten places was a Porsche.

Mercedes also tried to get its glory back in the 1988 race. Working with the Peter Sauber team from Switzerland, it entered two Sauber-Mercedes cars. Unfortunately, the Swiss-German machines had tire problems during practice and never made the starting grid. When they were out on the track, though, the vehicles showed tremendous speed and power.

The Sauber cars were design marvels—strong and lightweight. Their powerful twin-**turbocharged engines** came from the Mercedes sedan. But by the time the engines hit the track at Le Mans, they'd been pumped to produce nearly 700 horsepower!

Sauber body shapes were developed in the Mercedes-Benz wind tunnel, for best airflow. And the cars were finished in silver, Germany's classic racing color. They even took the same nickname Mercedes racers had used for years, the Silver Arrows.

In 1989 Sauber-Mercedes was determined to win, and it showed. The new C9 racers had the winning edge from day 1. When the checkered flag fell at Le Mans in June, a Mercedes was first to the finish line. The Silver Arrows had scored a bull's-eye!

In 1991 Jaguar, Porsche, and Mercedes battled again at Le Mans. But the race was won by a new car from a country Jaguar, Porsche, and Mercedes all feared.

For the first time, Le Mans was won by a Japanese car—a Mazda 787B. The car covered more than 3,000 miles in that single 24-hour period. Two more Mazdas finished in the top ten, in sixth and eighth places.

Japanese cars were not new to the race. Nissan, Mazda, and Toyota had entered cars before. They had also run their engines in European cars since the mid-1980s.

Japan's time on the winner's stand was short, however. Within a year, the race again had a French winner, as in the early 1970s. The giant Peugeot (POOH-joh) company brought the trophy back home in both 1992 and 1993.

Having a French car win the 1993 race was especially sweet for the ACO. It was the seventieth birthday of the race the club had started.

Sauber-Mercedes racers had gullwing doors like a 300SL.

THE TWENTY-FIFTH HOUR

Today Le Mans remains one of the world's most important races. Each June it attracts major carmakers and specialist builders alike. And, of course, it brings more than a quarter of a million fans to the track—as well as a worldwide TV audience.

What's in the future for this great event?

One trend has to do with combining Le Mans with other races. For years Le Mans was part of the World Sports Car championship. It was connected to races such as the Targa Florio in Italy and Nurburgring in Germany. Perhaps the best-known part of that famous series to Americans was the 12-hour race held each March in Sebring, Florida.

In recent years, though, a competing super-series has developed. It's the IMSA (International Motor Sports Association) series. And it's designed for prototype racing cars. IMSA races are held mostly at U.S. or Canadian tracks, including Daytona, Florida; Watkins Glen, New York; and Mosport Park in Canada.

43

Over the years, it's become too costly to compete in both European and IMSA series. So race officials are thinking about merging them. Don't be surprised to see IMSA cars racing at Le Mans one of these years.

Le Mans rules will continue to change. The track will change, too. Le Mans started out as an 11-mile course. And its form has changed 13 times over the years. The latest changes have been to put a couple of "kinks" into the Mulsanne to slow the cars to safer speeds. The track was also rebuilt in 1993 to improve safety. New barriers were added to reduce the risk of an accident like the 1955 disaster.

Le Mans, however, remains Le Mans. The greatest danger lies in having fast and slow cars on the same track in the dead of night. And that danger will be there as long as the race is open to different engine sizes.

The race cars themselves will continue to advance. Le Mans cars have always used the latest in technology, from disk brakes in the 1950s to ground effects today. The auto world is moving toward electronics and new materials. And Le Mans cars will put these new ideas to the test. If they can survive 24 hours of racing at 200-plus mph, they can probably survive anything!

In its way, Le Mans is still doing what it was designed to do. The race is improving the cars that ordinary folks drive or ride in every day. In that way, it's a track where *everyone* is out to win.

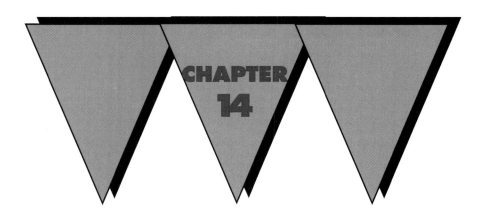

CHAPTER 14

SUNDAY, 4 P.M.

Since the crash, the shaking under your car has gotten worse. But some-how you know that the racing machine won't fail you now—it's taken you too far.

That's not so true for other drivers. Dead cars are all over the track. They litter the infield. Several are stuck in the sandbanks. Millions of dollars' worth of high-tech cars have been left at the roadside like abandoned junkers. It looks like a scene from a war movie.

Your car keeps going, though. You knew it would.

Then, almost as if the last 23 hours never happened, you're on the white-flag lap. No, you're not going to win, not this time. That honor will go to a factory team and to drivers who've raced here many times before. They're already on the winner's stand, surrounded by reporters and screaming fans.

No, you're not the winner. But you are going to finish the hardest, longest day in racing—the legendary Le Mans.

GLOSSARY

air brake A large panel that rises above the car and catches the air, slowing the car down. Air brakes were first used on Mercedes-Benz racers in 1955.

air-cooled engine An engine that is cooled by blowing air over it with a fan. This system replaces the usual liquid cooling system.

Autocross A sports-car contest in which the car races the clock through a course laid out with traffic cones.

Automobile Club de l'Ouest (ACO) The Auto Club of Western France, which created and sponsors the 24-hour Le Mans race.

boxer An engine in which the cylinders and pistons lie in a flat layout. The motion of the pistons is like two prizefighters jabbing away at each other.

chicane A kink or zigzag in a racecourse. Chicanes are put into straights to slow cars down to safer speeds.

disk brakes Brakes that have finger-like grippers that squeeze a disk attached to the wheel.

drum brakes Brakes that press on the insides of a drum attached to the wheel.

endurance The ability to do something physically difficult for a long time.

Grand Prix The French term for "Grand Prize." The term usually refers to a series of races featuring open-wheel cars.

ground effects Shaping of the underside of a car to create a vacuum over the road. Ground effects force the car to stick to the road on turns.

hemi An engine that uses round-topped (hemispherical) firing chambers. Chrysler hemi engines were used in many of the Cunningham race cars.

Index of Performance A category of Le Mans win awarded to the car that performed the best according to a formula based on engine size and distance. The Index of Performance is no longer awarded.

Indy A turn in the Le Mans course.

Le Mans start A way of starting a race in which the drivers line up and run to their parked cars before driving off. This start was used at Le Mans from 1923 through 1969, when it was banned for safety reasons.

Mulsanne Straight The 3-mile straight on the Le Mans course.

NASCAR (National Association for Stock Car Auto Racing) The group that controls most major stock car races in the United States.

open-wheel racer A car in which the wheels are on the outside of the body, completely exposed.

pace car A street vehicle that leads the race at the running start and slows the other cars during a caution.

prototype A specially built car designed to test out new ideas.

turbocharged engine An engine with a spinning, pumplike device that forces extra air-gas mixture into the engine, creating added power.

wind tunnel A scientific device used to see how a car's design acts when air flows over it at high speed.

INDEX